THE TENNIS

ALPHABET

A CELEBRATION OF TENNIS FROM A TO Z

by Kenneth G. Hess

photographs by Allen Kennedy

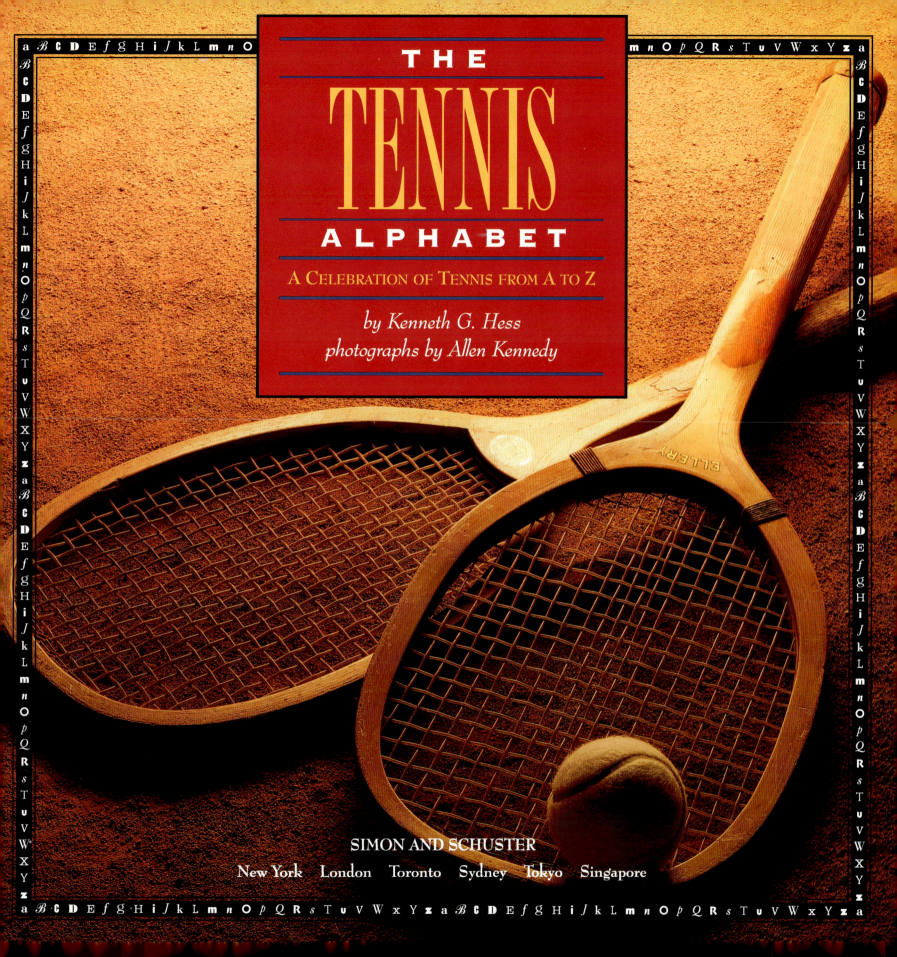

THE
TENNIS
ALPHABET

A CELEBRATION OF TENNIS FROM A TO Z

by Kenneth G. Hess
photographs by Allen Kennedy

SIMON AND SCHUSTER

New York London Toronto Sydney Tokyo Singapore

SIMON AND SCHUSTER
Simon & Schuster Building
Rockefeller Center
1230 Avenue of the Americas
New York, New York 10020

SIMON AND SCHUSTER and colophon are registered trademarks of Simon & Schuster Inc.

Designed by Kenneth G. Hess/SOMERSAULT BOOKS
Manufactured in the United States of America

1 3 5 7 9 10 8 6 4 2

Library of Congress Cataloging-in-Publication Data
Hess, Kenneth G.
The tennis alphabet : a celebration of tennis from A to Z / by Kenneth G. Hess ;
photographs by Allen Kennedy.
p. cm.
ISBN 0-671-74883-1 : $14.95
1. Tennis—Collectibles. 2. Tennis—Collectibles—Pictorial works. 3. Alphabet rhymes.
I. Title.
GV996.H47 1992   796.34'02—dc20   91-38343   CIP

To my first born son, Nicholas,

who reminds me so much of his dad.

I love you very much.

AUTHOR'S NOTE

The following rhymes are meant to be read aloud, whether to yourself or, preferably, to a large room of excitable players. Recite them in good health. Each of these magnificent photographs is both a tribute to the age old game of tennis and an illustration for your visual enjoyment. Savour them often.

a

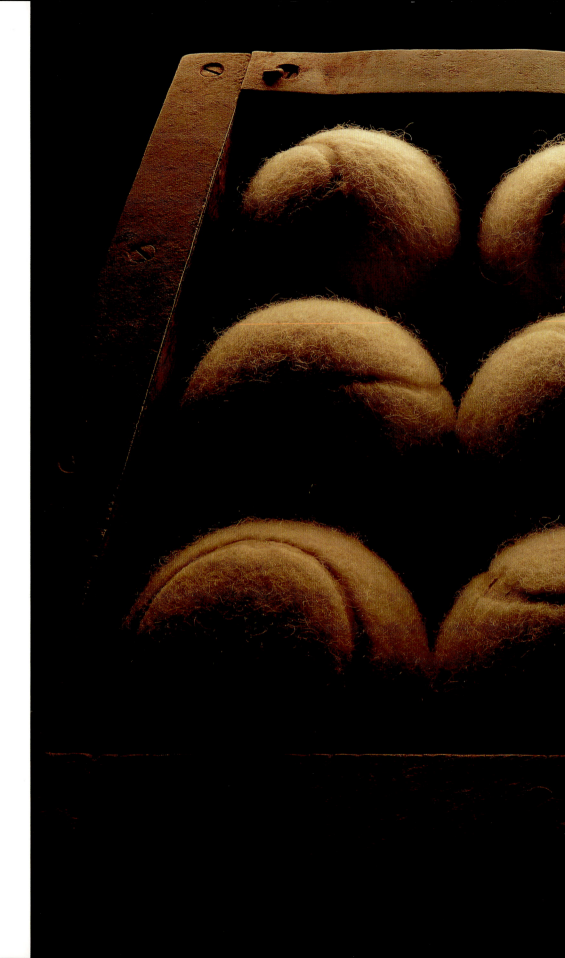

A is for Advantage.

It also stands for Ace.

Put them both together,

Your opponent's in disgrace.

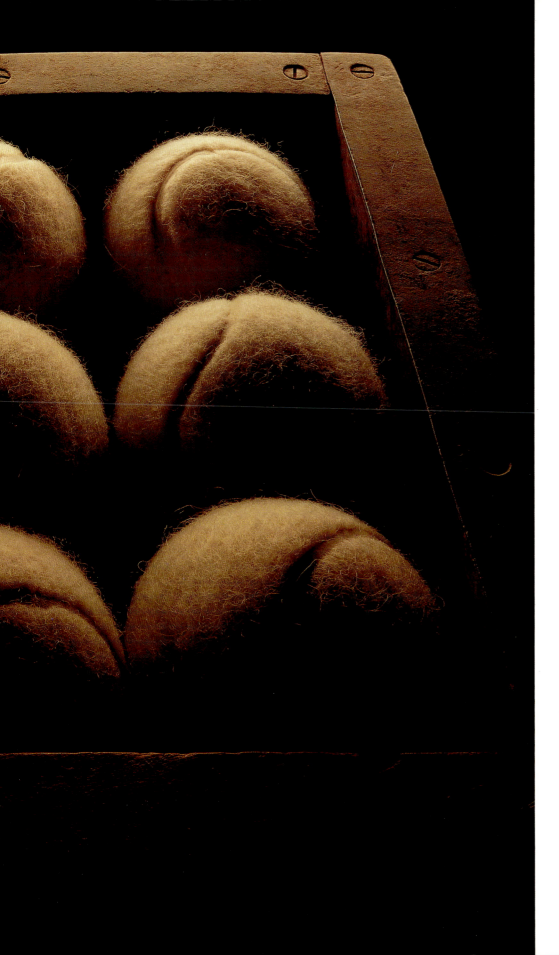

B is for those fuzzy Balls

That spin and slice about.

Who masters these will never fail

To champion every bout.

C

C is for the Change-of-pace

That always keeps them guessing.

A chop, a drop and some finesse,

They'll soon be acquiescing.

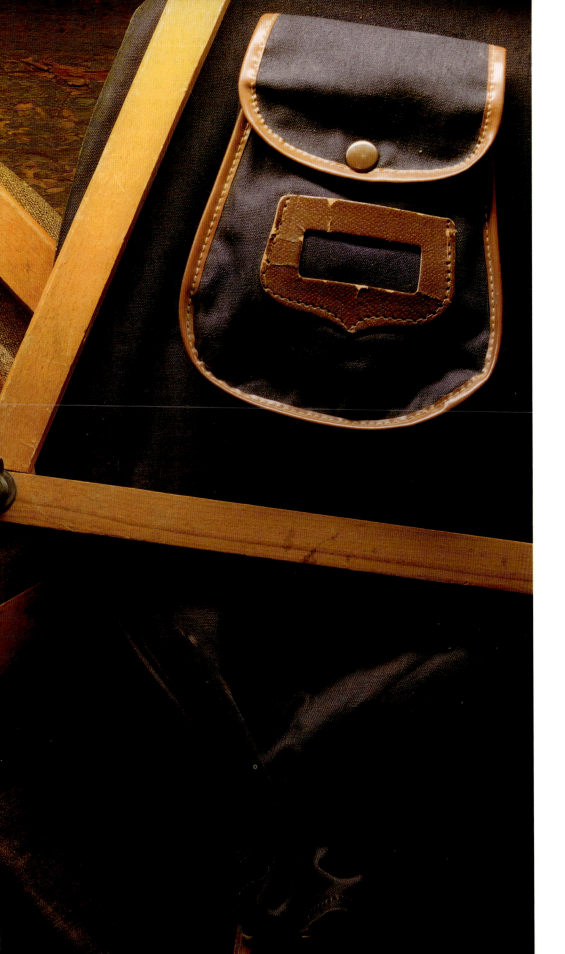

D is for that Doubles game.

It's a wonder you're not dead.

It seems your partner's only serve

Is a good bounce off your head.

E

E is for the Etiquette

Your opponent has forgotten.

It's the energy spent swearing

That has him playing rotten.

F is for the service "Fault!".

That word we loathe to hear,

From that blind nearsighted linesman

Whose voice we've learned to fear.

g

G is for the Game of Golf.

That sport of deprivations!

It's why we're playing tennis,

To throw off our frustrations.

H

H is for Half volleys

That always have you stumbling.

If one more ball hits at your feet,

You'll stumble off court mumbling.

i

I is for those Injuries

That seem to plague your stroking.

The problem though, is in your head.

It's known world-wide as choking.

J

J is for when you're "Just out!".

You've heard it once too often.

It seems that your opponent

Is out to nail your coffin.

k

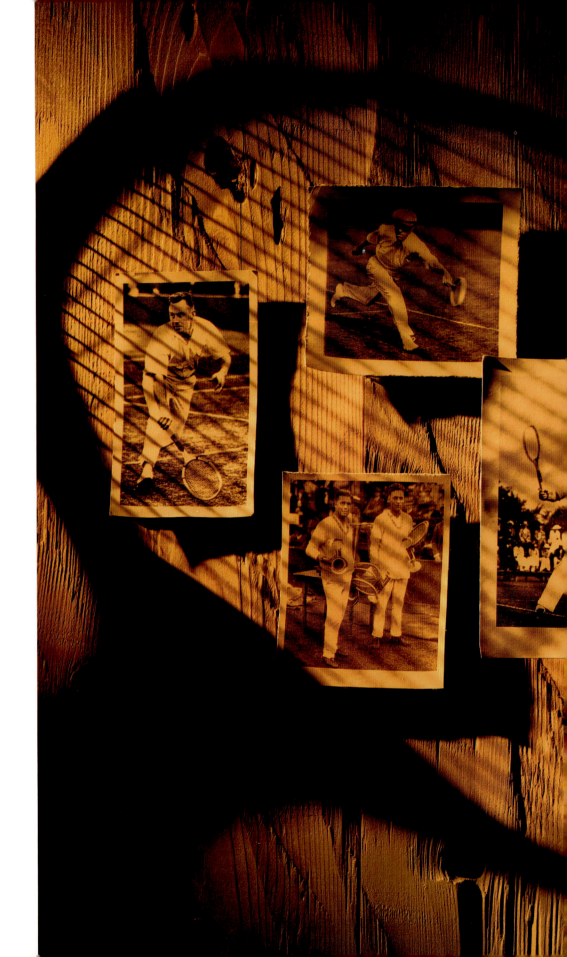

K is for that Knee of yours

That troubles you with pain.

Its kind of like that game of yours;

No wonder you complain.

L

L is for annoying Lets.

That test and fray your nerves.

Trouble is, they always come

At the end of your best serves.

m

M is for the Match point;

Monumental concentration.

Let's hope no one has noticed

You've got mental constipation.

n

N is for the Net play

You thought would help you win.

If only you remembered

That only fools rush in.

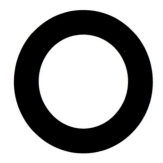

O is for the Overhead;

That smash we're mad about.

Especially when it turns the tide

And makes ad-in, ad-out.

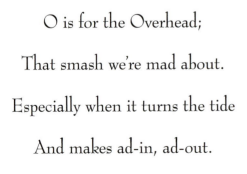

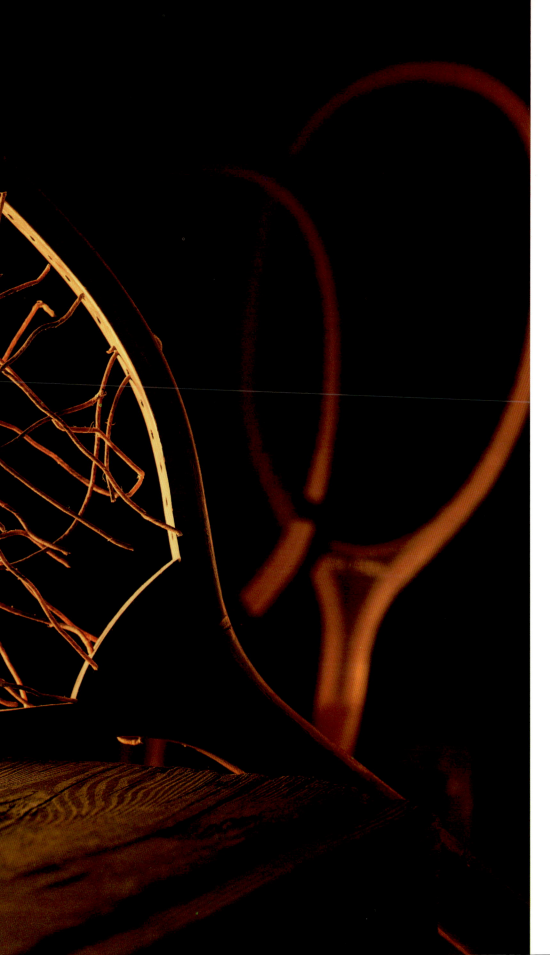

P

P is for your Partner,

Who doubles as your coach.

No matter what he tells you,

Your shots he's sure to poach.

Q

Q just stands for Quiet.

The silence 'round the service.

While meant to make us calmer,

Instead it makes us nervous.

J k L m n O p Q R s T u V W x

R is for the Racquet

That your opponent threw.

It seems his aim's improving

And so's his follow-through!

S

S is for your tennis Shoes.

They've sure enhanced your play.

Too bad the better that you get,

The more you'll have to pay.

T

T is for Tie-breaker

And Tense and Tired, too.

'Cuz after that long rally,

The one who'll break is you.

m n O p Q R s T v V W x Y z a

U

U is for the Umpires,

Those voices from above.

They call'em in, they call'em out,

But your favorite is "Six-Love".

V

V is for the Volley

That has you at the net.

Another dink like that one

And you'll psych this guy out, yet.

W

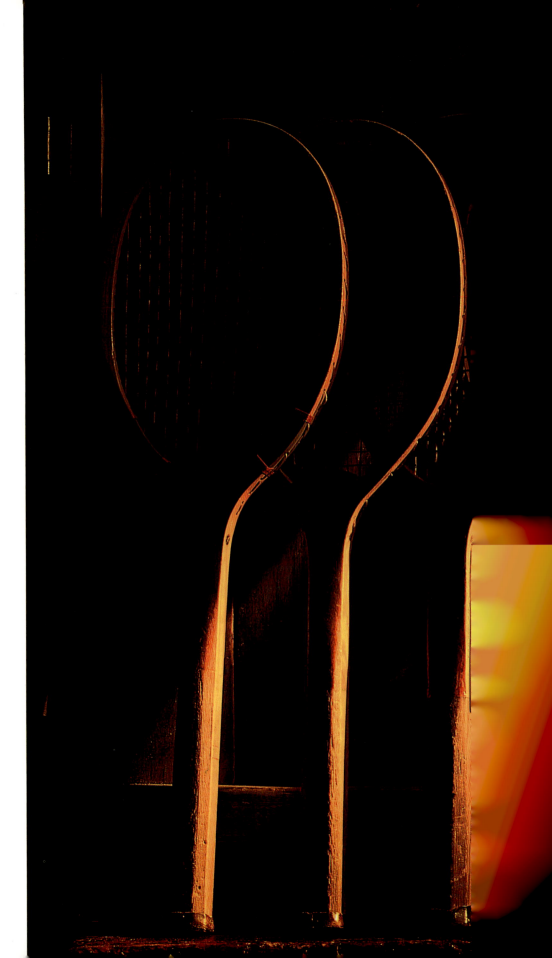

W's for the Winning drive.

That shot just blew her mind.

She thought you would go "forehand",

But it raced past her behind.

X

X now stands for cross(X)court.

It's the shot she'll use to win.

'Cuz no matter which she hits to,

It's the court that you're not in.

Y

Y is for the Yelling,

And the screaming and the cussing,

And the cursing and the swearing,

And the whining and the fussing.

R s T u V W x Y z a B C D E f

Z

Z is just for Zero.

But we say "l o v e" instead.

Its O.K. to love a little,

Love too much, though, and you're dead.

ACKNOWLEDGMENTS

The author and photographer would like to thank all of the people and organizations that helped make this book possible: Alan Kellock, Larry Lawrence, Somersault Books, Graphis Inc., Michael Weston, Patty Leasure, Joanne Barracca, Stacey Holsten, Jake Thamm, Tom Chenault (NuSkin), Bal Patterson of The Page book store on the Mall in Boulder, Simme Zelie, Katie Freytag, Jack McDonald, Becky Lenhart/The Colorado Tennis Association, Tectonic, The Snowmass Club, Kathleen Winegardner/The Clarion Harvest House in Boulder, Gilbert & Elanore Johnson, A.J. Hess, Ione Haynie and especially Sudi, Nicholas and Towner. You're the best.

Now, keep your eye on the ball and stop talking to yourself.